PENGUINS

PENGUINS

Annette Barkhausen and Franz Geiser

Gareth Stevens Publishing
MILWAUKEE

A N I M A L   F A M I L I E S

For a free color catalog describing Gareth Stevens's list of high-quality books, call 1-800-341-3569 (USA) or 1-800-461-9120 (Canada).

The series editor would like to extend special thanks to Edward N. Diebold, Curator of Birds at the Milwaukee County Zoological Gardens, Milwaukee, Wisconsin, for his kind and professional help with the information in this book.

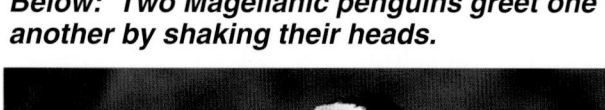

Below: Two Magellanic penguins greet one another by shaking their heads.

Library of Congress Cataloging-in-Publication Data

Barkhausen, Annette.
   [Pinguine. English]
   Penguins / by Annette Barkhausen and Franz Geiser; [translated from the German by Jamie Daniel]. — North American ed.
     p. cm. — (Animal families)
   Includes bibliographical references (p. 47) and index.
   Summary: An introduction to members of the penguin family, including chinstrap penguins, Fiordland penguins, and Macaroni penguins.
   ISBN 0-8368-1002-3
   1. Penguins—Juvenile literature. [1. Penguins.] I. Geiser, Franz. II. Title. III. Series: Animal families (Milwaukee, Wis.)
   QL696.S473B3413 1993
   598.4'41—dc20   93-13050

Above: Emperor penguins will be able to return to the sea only when their new feathers have grown in completely.

North American edition first published in 1994 by
Gareth Stevens Publishing
1555 North RiverCenter Drive, Suite 201
Milwaukee, Wisconsin 53212, USA

Series editor: Patricia Lantier-Sampon
Editor: Barbara J. Behm
Translated from the German by Jamie Daniel
Editorial assistants: Diane Laska and Andrea Schneider
Editorial consultant: Edward N. Diebold

Printed in Mexico

1 2 3 4 5 6 7 8 9 98 97 96 95 94

Table of Contents

Picture Credits

A.G.E.—7 (lower), 10 (upper), 12 (upper), 13 (Adélie Penguin, Chinstrap Penguin, King Penguin), 15 (lower); Coleman—Fennell 39 (right): Frances 32, 33; Dossenbach—4 (left); Editoy—40; EMB Archive—6, 7 (upper); IFA—BCl 24: Berger 9 (upper and lower), 18 (right): Gottschalk 25: Graf 26: Prenzel 13 (Little Blue Penguin), 38; Jacana—Ferrero 20 (left), 23 (left): Gohier 20 (right), 21, 28: Hawkes 18 (left): Montes 14: Prevost 15 (upper), 16 (right); Suinot title page, 4-5, 16 (left): Trouillet 12 (lower): Varin 39 (left): Varin-Visage 8 (lower), 23 (right): Winner 8 (upper); NHPA—Bannister 27: Hawkes 4 (right): Johnson 19, 22, 34: Scott 10 (lower); Reinhard—1, 2, 11, 13 (Galápagos Penguin), 17, 29, 30, 31, 39 (left); Wartmann—13 (Macaroni Penguin, Yellow-Eyed Penguin), 35, 36, 37.

What Is a Penguin?

Opposite, top: "They [the seafarers] took 50,000 of these birds" is the short description written for this etching from the year 1633.

The English navy lieutenant William Clayton was surprised and confused. He had seen animals on the Falkland Islands in the south Atlantic Ocean that reminded him of birds, mammals, and fish all at the same time. That was over two hundred years ago. Clayton wrote in a report at that time: "These creatures live primarily in the sea. They have very short wings that serve as flippers, and they are covered with short, thick feathers. They swim at astonishingly high speeds. On land, they march upright at a wobbly pace. From far away, they look like children who have toddled out into the snow wearing white aprons and bibs. In October, they come up on the land to lay and incubate their eggs. All of their eggs taste good and are very nutritious, a wonderful treat for seafarers. And yet the flesh of these animals is tough. It has a fishy taste and isn't suitable for eating."

Discovered and Then Exploited

European explorers saw penguins for the first time toward the end of the fifteenth century. Not long after this, penguin eggs were found in the cooking pots of sailors, and penguin fat was being turned into lamp oil. About 1 pint (.5 liter) of oil could be processed from the 3/4-inch-(2-centimeter) thick layer of fat found under the skin of an emperor penguin. Macaroni and royal penguins were just as rich in oil. The most famous penguin oil factory was built on the Macquarie Islands of New Zealand. There, 150,000 royal penguins were killed for their oil every year between 1894 and 1914.

Penguins live only in the Earth's Southern Hemisphere. Most of the seventeen species of penguins live on the islands surrounding the continent of Antarctica, as well as on the Antarctic coastline. Some also live in the warmer areas along the coasts of Australia, South America, and southern Africa.

How Penguins Evolved

Scientists cannot identify the direct ancestors of penguins. But these ancestors must have been birds that could fly. The nearest relatives to penguins in the bird kingdom are petrels and albatrosses. It is possible that these flying birds share a common ancestor with the penguins.

English captain Sir James Ross saw emperor penguins in 1842. He was the first European to sail into what is now called the Ross Sea.

adapted completely to the sea a million years ago. This was probably because of a lack of land predators. The power of flight was no longer necessary.

In prehistoric times, the ancestors of the penguins had to either give up flying or give up the sea as a source of food. Slowly, they began to change physically so as to stay in close touch with their source of food. Their long wing bones evolved into short, flattened-out bones. Their wings became flippers.

Gaining flippers is not enough to account for the level of adaptation that today's penguins have reached. The entire body had to become streamlined for easy movement through the water. In addition, the many air

Penguins are unusual birds. They cannot fly in the air (although they use their flippers to "fly" underwater), and they are not very steady on land with their strange, wobbly walk. Even so, they seem to make their way through life with great success. Penguins

pockets that are found in the bones of other birds had to be eliminated.

A penguin's feathers are distributed evenly over its entire body. No gaps exist between the feathers, as they do in most bird species. They are round at the tip and very soft at the base. The soft feathers, called *down*, keep a warm layer of air trapped next to the penguin's skin. The outer sections of the feathers are layered over one another like scales to form a watertight skin. Under the feathers is a layer of fat. The fat reserve probably differs from species to species. Scientists argue over whether the fat layer serves as insulation or as an energy source.

Below: These king penguins have finally reached their destination — the sea!

Bottom: Penguins are completely at home under the water. Their bodies are streamlined and offer little resistance to the water. They can reach speeds of several miles (kilometers) per hour, powered by their flippers.

Below: Social life among the penguins. A male king penguin announces his interest in finding a mate by raising his head high.

Bottom: A brooding penguin greets its partner, who has returned after a few days of feeding at sea.

The remains of early penguins have been found on the coasts of New Zealand and Australia — some over 45 million years old. Some early penguins that populated the area 20 to 30 million years later were similar in height and weight to today's humans. The largest penguin today, the emperor penguin, is only about 3 feet (1 meter) tall and weighs an average of about 65 pounds (30 kg).

Master Divers and Swimmers

The change from flying to swimming birds was beneficial for the penguins. Today, they are among the best divers and swimmers in the animal kingdom. Chinstrap penguins dive to depths of 230 feet (70 m), gentoo penguins to 358 feet (109 m), and king penguins to 787 feet (240 m) or more. The master diver among the penguins is the emperor penguin. It can dive to 870 feet (265 m) and remain underwater for eighteen minutes. It can also reach a swimming speed of up to 9 miles (15 km) an hour. Why the emperor is such an outstanding diver and swimmer is a mystery. Scientists do not know how the bird can store up enough oxygen for such a long dive or how it exhales under water the harmful gases produced in its body. Emperor penguins swim faster and dive deeper, longer, and more often than scientists consider possible.

Except for the nesting period when penguins start a family, the sea is their home. Many, especially the younger birds, wander far and wide in the sea in search of food. Little blues and yellow-eyed penguins, however, stay in their breeding area all year long.

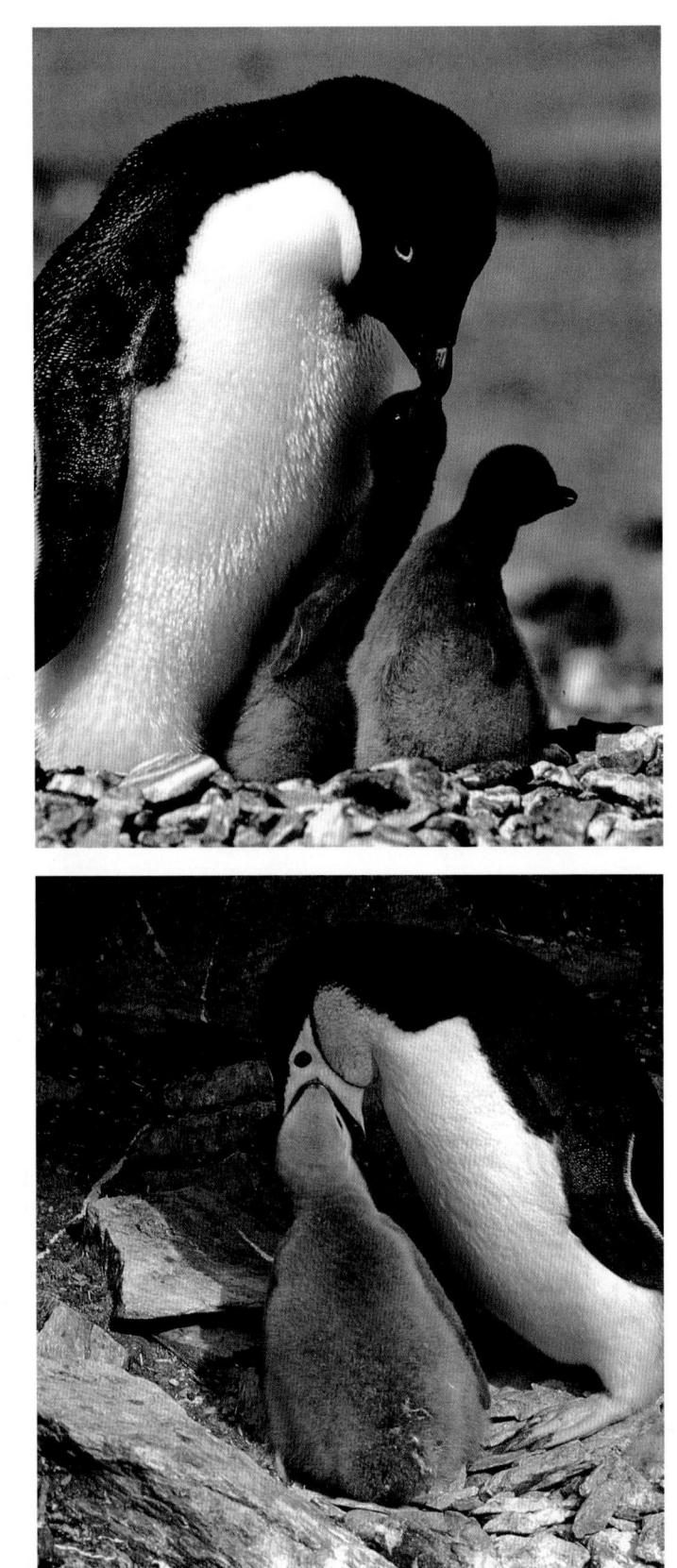

Predigested krill is the main source of nourishment for many young penguins. This is true for both the Adélie (left) and the chinstrap (below) penguins.

Brooding, Calling, and Fasting

In September or October, when it is springtime in the Southern Hemisphere, most species of penguin head for their brooding or nesting sites. Entire colonies of penguins arise from the sea. The males must claim and occupy a nesting place in order for the females to be attracted to them. All of this takes place with a deafening amount of noise. Penguins like to call, even if their "calling" sounds to humans like a cross between a trumpet blaring and a donkey neighing. To penguins, however, this call is extremely important. Each species has its own distinctive call. In addition, each bird performs its personal version of its particular species' call.

In the large nesting colonies, called *rookeries*, there are up to one million penguins gathered in a crowded space — all of them looking very much alike. This presents a problem for each individual penguin. The male must claim a nesting place within this enormous throng which will be clearly acknowledged as his very own by the other birds. In addition, he has to make himself noticeable to potential mates within the enormous crowd.

Each penguin must be able to defend itself in order to keep intruders out of its nesting area. Penguins divide the labor during chick brooding. Without cooperation between both of its parents, no offspring would survive. The penguin language of gestures and calls helps them live together relatively peacefully, even in the larger colonies. The penguins call the most during the mating and nesting

Below, left: Temperatures around the freezing point are too warm for an Adélie penguin. It spreads its wings to release excess internal body heat.

Below, right: A king penguin during the molting, or shedding, season.

Bottom: Birds called sheathbills (Chionis alba) are unwelcome guests in this king penguin colony. The sheathbills eat penguin eggs and chicks and snatch food away from hungry young penguins.

egg incubation on an empty stomach. First, the nest must be prepared for eggs. Smaller penguins lay two eggs; larger emperor and king penguins lay just one. After the eggs are laid, one parent can return to the sea to eat. The other remains with the eggs and incubates them until his or her partner returns.

The most stressful period for the parents begins once the young penguins have hatched. The little ones are constantly hungry and must be fed with the regurgitated contents of their parents' stomachs. This can include krill, shrimp, fish, or squid. The young must be guarded constantly, or they will fall victim to aerial predators such as sheathbills or

periods. Male penguins that already occupy a nest cry out their desire to find a mate. With their backs arched, the males raise their heads, flutter their wings, and sometimes accentuate the display with a trumpeting cry. This display usually meets with success. The female arrives and competing males know enough to stay away. Pairs reinforce their bond in a similar fashion. They stand facing each other, raise their heads up high and call without interruption. In this way, they learn to recognize the particular individual voices of their partners. Only emperor penguins seem to be shy with one another. They sing together with their heads bowed toward one another's feet.

In spite of this elaborate courtship behavior, penguins must get on with the business of raising a family. Time is important because most penguins carry out the task of

![Killer whale breaching in the water with an island in the background]

Above: Killer whales sometimes eat larger penguins. However, sea lions are much more likely to attack penguins.

giant petrels. The sheathbill tries to get between the parent and the baby during feeding time to steal regurgitated food. This bird will also look for a chance to steal unguarded eggs.

Soon, however, young penguins are big and healthy enough to be left alone while their parents return to the sea to hunt for food. Many species of Antarctic penguin, such as Adélie, chinstrap, emperor, king, and rockhopper penguins, gather their young into groups, called *crèches*, while the adults hunt. The young are fed only by their own parents.

At about seven to eight weeks of age, the penguin chicks get their first coat of feathers to replace their soft down coats. The little penguins do not go into the water until all down has been shed.

Left: Penguins often decorate postage stamps in various countries.

king penguin

Galápagos penguin

chinstrap penguin

macaroni penguin

yellow-eyed penguin

A Guide to Penguins

little blue penguin

Adélie penguins

Emperor Penguins

Scientific name: Aptenodytes forsteri
Total length: 45 inches (115 cm)
Weight (average): 66 pounds (30 kg)

Emperor penguins choose the icy southern continent of Antarctica for their nesting areas. They bring their young into the world in the middle of winter. Because it is so cold, there is almost no water available. And there is so little food on land that all of the larger animals living there — seals and penguins — must get their food from the sea.

When the long, pitch-dark polar nights begin in March, several thousand pairs of emperor penguins gather on the Antarctic ice. They come directly from their fishing grounds in the sea and are well nourished.

Once on land, the emperors mate, fast, and lay eggs. The female lays a single egg that weighs about 17.7 ounces (500 grams). The egg can never rest directly on the ice because the cold would kill the life inside of it. A few hours after the egg is laid, the female turns it over to the male. The two birds form a bridge between them with their webbed feet. Over this bridge, the female gently rolls the egg to the male. The male then protects it in his warm stomach pouch. The egg rests on top of the feet, covered by an abdominal flap.

This process leaves the female emperors free. Exhausted after two months of fasting and the effort of laying eggs, female penguins head for the sea to eat. However, during this time, a stretch of coastline water 50 to 93 miles (80 to 150 km) wide has frozen. So, before the females can get to the fish, they must cross this distance, waddling on their short legs and sliding on their bellies.

The males must remain back on shore, warming the eggs on their feet. They stand there for two months, constantly turning the

eggs that cannot be allowed to get any colder than 86° F (30° C) — even though the air temperature is -22° F (-30° C) or colder! If a sudden Antarctic snowstorm comes up, with winds that can reach speeds up to 87 miles (140 km) an hour, the male penguins huddle close together. They huddle so close that the wind reaches only about one-fifth of their entire body surface.

The emperor penguin is well equipped to deal with this cold. Its skin has twelve feathers per .155 sq. inch (1 sq. cm.). The scalelike top sections of these feathers overlap to form a waterproof, weatherproof shell. Underneath this shell is a fine, furlike layer of down.

Right, top: "Shall we walk together, my friend?"

Bottom, right: The feather "coat" of the emperor penguin keeps it warm.

Bottom, left: Using personalized calls, emperor penguins can find their mates.

During the mating and brooding period, when the penguins prepare for the eggs to hatch, male emperor penguins don't eat anything. They must, therefore, conserve as much energy as possible. Because of this, they don't move any more than necessary. They spend most of their time standing in one place dozing. In spite of this, they still lose about a third of their body weight.

on their bodies. In spite of this, they must make the long journey across the ice to the sea in order to feed on fish. They have two weeks to eat their fill. Then they must return with food for the hungry little ones.

The parent penguins continue to take turns returning to feed in the sea. The

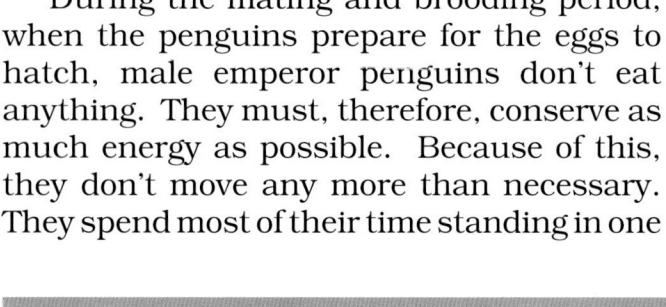

place dozing. In spite of this, they still lose about a third of their body weight.

Finally, after sixty-four days, penguin chicks hatch from the eggs. Then the females return, their bellies stuffed with fish. In their gullets, they carry about 7 pounds (3 kg) of food for the newly hatched chicks. Their arrival doesn't come a moment too soon to feed the hungry offspring. The males are not able to offer the young such a feast. They are now so thin that their skin sometimes sags

hatching and raising of the chicks takes about six months. Generally speaking, the larger a bird is, the longer the period of time necessary for raising their young. The smaller Adélie penguins, for example, can raise their young in half the time as the emperors.

Top, left: An adult emperor protects its chick.

Top, right: Older emperor penguin chicks live in groups. But they are fed only by their parents.

Opposite: Two king penguins mating.

16

King Penguins

Scientific name: Aptenodytes patagonica
Total length: 37.5 inches (95 cm)
Weight: 33 pounds (15 kg)

King penguins are similar to the emperors, except for the colorful markings on their head and breast. The spot behind their ears is particularly striking. It plays an important role when males try to catch the attention of the females during the mating season. During this time, the male announces his interest in mating by stretching his back and raising his head up high. The female then approaches the male to get a better look. After a period of looking each other over, the male penguin stands up as straight as he can and marches in front of his partner. As he marches, he turns his head back and forth from left to right so that she can marvel at the full effect of his orange ear markings. If she decides to follow him, they will soon mate and raise a chick together.

The brooding and chick-rearing period of the king penguins is similar to that of the emperors, except that it takes place more directly on the coast of Antarctica as well as on small islands in the southern polar sea. As is the case for the emperors, the female king penguin will lay only one egg. But since the king penguins lay eggs close to the water, they don't have to travel great distances to find food. Thus, the males and females can leave the brood site more frequently than the emperors. In addition, the chicks hatch after just fifty-four days, ten days earlier than the eggs of the emperors. The most important difference between the two species is the time of year they choose for breeding. The emperor incubates its eggs during the middle of winter. This makes it possible for the young to be hatched in spring. Therefore, the young grow up during the brief polar summer when the

sea offers the greatest nourishment. The king penguins, however, lay their eggs in spring (like many of the smaller species of penguin) and then incubate in summer. The chicks hatch in late summer. Unlike the smaller Adélie penguins, the kings don't have enough time to grow up during the brief

summer. They are only half-grown by winter. They must brave icy winter storms huddled close together in groups. It is hard for the parents to get enough food to their offspring during this time. The young king penguins are finally grown enough to be on their own in the spring when their parents molt, or shed, their feathers.

The reproductive cycle of the king penguins lasts about fifteen months. This means that the brooding sequence varies. It changes by

In the nineteenth century, king penguins were ruthlessly hunted for their oil. This slaughter reduced the king penguin population greatly. Their numbers began to increase again only in the twentieth century.

The king penguins' diving record is about 787 feet (240 m). In addition, the king penguin reaches a remarkable speed in the water of 5.3 miles (8.5 km) an hour.

the bright sky. From above, their black backs serve the same purpose, since they cannot be seen against the dark ocean depths. They are protected from predators both above and below the water.

The two larger penguins, emperors and kings, are the best divers of all the penguins. They typically raise two chicks every three years. They must wait six months to breed again. They are not able to start a new brood right away. They have molted in the fall, the parents are not

On land, king penguins present a very formal appearance. With their black "tuxedo jackets" and white "shirts," they look as if they have been invited to a formal affair. These markings serve as camouflage. From below the surface of the water, the penguins' white bellies can hardly be recognized against

three months every second year. Parents that have bred in the spring of the previous year are not free to raise new offspring until the summer. The second penguin chick enters the harsh winter period at a very young age and is self-sufficient only late in the following summer. After their feathers

Adélie Penguins

Scientific name: Pygoscelis adeliae
Total length: 27.5 inches (70 cm)
Weight: 11 pounds (5 kg)

The Adélie penguin is the best known and the most common of all the penguin species that live on the Antarctic continent.

In October, when spring comes to the South Pole, the Adélies are ready to mate. They leave the sea for their ancestral rookeries. The journey is hard to make even at this time of year, for the sea around Antarctica is frozen. The little Adélies must sometimes walk up to 62 miles (100 km) over the ice before they finally reach their destination. They can cover 3 miles (5 km) an hour on foot, but this pace is too slow. So they throw themselves down and slide across the ice on their bellies. This is called *tobogganing*.

The male Adélies are the first to arrive at the rookeries. Older brooding birds will immediately re-occupy their customary nest sites. But even young birds are soon able to establish places for themselves. Once they have reached the age of six or seven, they will nest for the first time.

Once a male bird has occupied a nesting site, he will announce his success with the typical penguin gesture of raising his head to the sky. The meaning of this gesture is not lost on passing females. The females will select a mate from the pool of eligible males. If a female encounters a male with whom she mated the year before, she will prefer to mate with him again. As soon as the female Adélie has laid her two eggs, she will return to the sea to eat. The parents see each other only a few times more while taking turns at the nest.

Opposite: After a 54-day brooding period (left), emperor penguin parents must feed the chicks for another month (right).

Adélie penguins lay their eggs in nests of pebbles they build themselves. It is especially important for them to have enough pebbles gathered if they are brooding on snow. If only a few stones are available, the parent's body warmth will melt the snow beneath the eggs, and the cold will kill the unborn chicks. Thus both parents are constantly occupied with

This lone adult acts as a supervisor for a group of Adélie chicks.

gathering enough pebbles. The male is the principle nest builder before the eggs are laid. The male will concern himself with stones once again after the nest is established and he is taking his turn going to the sea. There is a multitude of pebbles in the world, but there are never enough of them in Adélie colonies. Because of this, Adélies have become skilled thieves. They will pretend to be poking around in the areas between strangers' nests, but really they are waiting for the chance to steal. But this behavior usually doesn't fool their brooding neighbors for a minute. The

tries to get food from an adult that is not its parent will be chased away. Chicks are fed only by their own parents, and no one else. Even the so-called supervisors of the groups don't stand too close to the chicks. Birds without mates usually act as supervisors.

After the thaw of summer, only a few

neighbors drive the intruder away with opened beaks. But sometimes the thief is successful. When no one is looking, he snatches a stone and hurries back to his own nest.

After a 34-day incubation period, the two Adélie chicks hatch. The chicks must be guarded and warmed by one of their parents for another three weeks. The other Adélie partner will meanwhile fill his or her gullet with krill in the sea to nourish the hungry chicks. In time, the chicks grow larger and more self-sufficient. They stay together in groups. Up to one hundred young Adélies will stand clustered close together, waiting for food. As the parents return, they announce their arrival with loud cries. Their offspring answer them immediately. And a chick that

icebergs remain bobbing in the water. It is time for the Adélies' favorite game. Bird after bird hops onto a passing chunk of ice and lets itself be carried along for a short while. Then the birds hop off and swim back to their point of departure, ready to board the next passing ice "boat."

Except when they are breeding, the Adélies are on the move. Researchers Richard Penney and John Emlen wanted to know how these

Above, left: Young Adélies share warm regards.

Above, right: Certain greeting games help make the relationships between Adélie mates closer.

Opposite: Because of dangerous sea lions, Adélie penguins enter the sea in groups.

penguins find their way around. They captured five birds and then released them 2,360 miles (3,800 km) away from their rookery. Ten months later, the penguins were back on their breeding grounds, having traveled an average of 18.7 miles (30 km) every day. The Adélies probably use the Sun as their guide, because they seem to wander aimlessly when the sky is overcast. But when the Sun is shining and they are in an unfamiliar location, they will always head in a more or less northerly direction, away from the South Pole. This way, they always reach the sea, the source of their food.

Gentoo Penguins

Scientific name: Pygoscelis papua
Total length: 29.5 inches (75 cm)
Weight: 13 pounds (6 kg)

Anyone who has ever visited a colony of gentoo penguins will understand why they are called "mule" penguins in German. They make a terrible braying sound together, just like a giant herd of mules. Gentoos live on the coasts of the Antarctic continent and on many islands in the southern oceans. Gentoos in a particular region will remain all year long in their rookery and have almost no contact with gentoos from other regions. Because of this, two subspecies of gentoo have developed

Above: *Gentoo penguins like nothing better than marching off together into the sea.*

Young penguins can live off the huge schools of krill that appear along the coastline during summer. The chicks grow slowly and eat about 265 pounds (120 kg) of krill before they are grown. By way of comparison, Adélie penguins need to supply only 110 pounds (50 kg) of krill for their chicks. Southern gentoo penguins can usually find more food than the gentoos that live farther north. Because of this, they don't have to leave their chicks for as long a time as northern gentoos do.

over the years. The subspecies differ in bill, flipper, and foot measurements as well as breeding times and eating habits. The southern gentoos have smaller bills, flippers, and feet, probably an adaptation for heat conservation in the colder climate.

Like their Adélie relatives, Antarctic gentoo penguins brood in September and October.

In the Crozet Islands, off the coast of southern Africa, gentoos lay their eggs in July. The two eggs are incubated for thirty-five or thirty-six days, and rearing of the chicks takes about two months. The last of the young birds are ready to be on their own in the sea in January, making it possible for the adults to molt in February. Other gentoos

Female gentoos lay two eggs, which both parents take turns incubating for about thirty-three days. The penguins look for food in coastal waters. Food supplies vary from island to island. The chicks are fed fish, krill and other shrimp, squid, or even worms.

There are 300,000 pairs of gentoos altogether in the world. Three-quarters of

living on islands brood in early winter, in February or March. They prefer nesting sites in areas with a good cover of green plants, which they use as nesting material. The penguins alternate their nesting sites every few years so nature has a chance to replenish the plant cover.

Above, left: Gentoos are able to raise two chicks only if they have a sufficient food supply.

Above, right: A gentoo guards its eggs closely.

these live on three islands or island groups: the Falklands, South Georgia Island, and Kerguelen Island.

Gentoo penguins are charming creatures and are rarely aggressive. They have a well-developed sense of how to get along in society. Once a day, they march together in a long column to the sea and take a quick swim together. In the afternoon, they all head back home to their nesting sites.

Chinstrap Penguins

Scientific name: Pygoscelis antarctica
Total length: 27 inches (68 cm)
Weight: 10 pounds (4.5 kg)

difficult, steep areas, they climb along, holding on to the rocks with their beaks and claws.

The chinstrap breeding season begins in October or November. The birds leave the sea and its nourishment and return to both the same nesting site and the same mate they had the previous year.

Chinstraps are fearless penguins. There are a great many chinstrap penguins, but they can only be found on Antarctica and on several nearby islands. In their enormous rookeries, they communicate by means of an ear-piercing cry. They have been known to drive human beings away by raising their beaks and flapping their wings. When chinstraps brood near other species of penguin, they prefer to claim the higher areas. They are quite skilled at climbing up cliffs and hopping from rock to rock. In

Female chinstraps usually lay two eggs on bare rock — only a few pebbles keep them from rolling away. If the rookery has a shortage of space, some penguins brood on the snow. The eggs hatch in the middle of the Antarctic summer in January after a 35-day incubation period. Unfortunately, gulls and other birds known as sheathbills sometimes attack the chicks and their food.

Above: Chinstrap penguins must sit on their eggs longer than Adélies or gentoos, but their chicks grow up faster once they have hatched.

Magellanic Penguins

Scientific name: Spheniscus magellanicus
Total length: 27.5 inches (70 cm)
Weight: 8.8 pounds (4 kg)

not always happen at the same times, however. This means that the penguins sometimes arrive at their breeding grounds hungry. Often, one partner in a pair will not be able to bear the hunger until he or she is relieved by the other bird. It will then give up the nesting site and return to the sea. When this happens,

Magellanic penguins inhabit the Pacific and Atlantic coasts of southern South America. In August and September, they migrate from northerly wintering regions back to the rookery in the southern areas. There, the Magellanic pairs seek out their old nesting places, usually burrows dug into the ground. The female lays two eggs in October, and the chicks hatch a month later. The chicks are fully grown after about ten weeks.

Adult Magellanic penguins primarily eat small fish. The migrations of fish schools do

the birds will not nest again for awhile, even if the food situation improves in the meantime. Since these penguins live a long time and are able to breed for many years, this doesn't have a dangerous effect on the population. There are enough Magellanic penguins to survive such situations — provided, that is, they don't meet an early death at the hands of oil merchants or in fishing nets.

Above: The parent protects the chicks in the nest from attacks by gulls.

Peruvian Penguins

Scientific name: Spheniscus humboldti
Total length: 25.5 inches (65 cm)
Weight: 9.3 pounds (4.2 kg)

Peruvian penguins, also referred to as Humboldt penguins, live on the coasts of Peru and Chile in South America. Sometimes their breeding grounds overlap with those of their close relatives, the Magellanic penguins. It is easy to distinguish between the two because of neck markings. Peruvian penguins have one broad black-and-white band on their neck, while Magellanic penguins have two white and two black bands on their neck.

Ocean currents bring cold water from the Antarctic to the surface along the western coast of South America. Enormous schools of fish that provide the main source of food for penguins inhabit these waters. Occasionally, a warm sea current called *El Niño* interrupts. When the warm water overcomes the colder Humboldt Current, the penguins go hungry.

While Magellanic penguins do not brood in such years, Peruvian penguins can adjust to a scarcer food source. Peruvian penguins have several brooding periods each year. If the penguins lose their first nest, they will try a second time.

Peruvian penguins have trouble finding a suitable nesting place. They once built their nests in burrows in plentiful piles of dried guano. Guano is the excrement of thousands of generations of seabirds left along the South American coastline. In some places, there once were layers of guano over 100 feet (30 m) thick. But humans use guano as fertilizer. Today's low numbers of Peruvian penguins are probably a result of the exploitation of guano by people. Penguins must now limit themselves to natural cavities in the rocks or burrows in the earth and sand.

Peruvian penguins lay two eggs. Parents share the duties of raising the chicks. During incubation and for as long as the chicks are small, one parent always stays at the nest. Later, the parents go out together in search of food. They swim with wide-open beaks into schools of little fish. As is the case for other

penguin species, the tongues and gums of the Peruvian penguins are equipped with little prongs that help keep hold of the fish and guide them down their throats.

Above: Peruvian penguins groom each other's head feathers as a sign of affection.

African Penguins

Scientific name: Spheniscus demersus
Total length: 27.5 inches (70 cm)
Weight: 6.5 pounds (3 kg)

In the year 1499, Portuguese explorer Vasco da Gama tried to find a sea route to India. India could not be reached by ship at that time — the Suez Canal did not yet exist. Da Gama thus chose the long sea journey around the southern tip of Africa. It was on this voyage of discovery that Europeans saw penguins for the first time — the African, or black-footed, penguins. One sailor reported this encounter as follows: ". . . saw birds as big as ganders. Their cry sounds like that of a mule, and they are unable to fly."

In spite of their having been discovered at that early date, very little is known about the African penguins. They live on the coasts and small islands around the southern tip of Africa. Their habitat extends from Angola on the western coast of Africa as far as Mozambique on the eastern coast. In the past, they lived mainly in guano hollows. But this type of shelter has disappeared for the same reasons it has for the Peruvian penguin — people have carried away the guano to sell for fertilizer. Today, many African penguins brood in nests on the bare ground.

African penguins do not have a set nesting period, but the most intense nesting activity takes place in November and in March. They seek shelter in hollows, in self-dug burrows in the sand, or beneath the scarce plant cover. The female bird lays two eggs that are incubated in turns by both parents for about forty days. The penguins' main source of food — schools of small fish — can be found not far from their rookeries along the coast. They must also watch out for sharks and other marine predators that like to feed on penguins.

In the past, commercial egging led to dramatic declines in the numbers of African penguins. And, because they eat fish, African penguins are a nuisance to the fishing industry. Commercial fishing has also reduced the penguins' food supply. But oil spills are probably the most serious

contemporary threat for this species. Current population estimates approximate fifty thousand to eighty thousand pairs of African penguins. This species formerly numbered in the millions.

Above: Everybody in! The water's fine!

27

Galápagos Penguins

Scientific name: Spheniscus mendiculus
Total length: 21 inches (53 cm)
Weight: 5 pounds (2.2 kg)

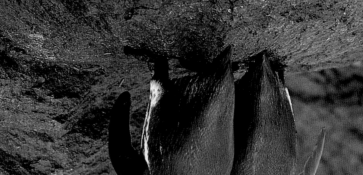

Galápagos penguins live in an unlikely environment — at the Equator! Their rookeries are not cold or covered by ice or snow. But even though the Galápagos penguins inhabit a hot, tropical region, they still have a connection with the Antarctic. The Galápagos islands lie along the Humboldt Current, which brings cold, food-filled water to the penguins from the Antarctic.

The tropical habitat causes some problems for the Galápagos penguins. The water in which they fish is somewhat cool, with a temperature that fluctuates between 59° and 83° F (15° and 28° C). But the air temperature on the Galápagos Islands, which reaches 104° F (40° C), poses a special threat to the penguins. They cannot always succeed in finding shady hollows to stay in. When this

The Galápagos penguin is smaller than its closest relatives, the African, Peruvian, and Magellanic penguins. Its head is almost all black with a narrow band of white around its cheeks. It is the rarest type of penguin. There are apparently only between one thousand and three thousand of these birds alive.

happens, the birds must stand in the hot Sun in their feather coats and suffer the heat. Like all other penguins, they need a thick, watertight coat of feathers for swimming. And under this, they have an insulating layer of fat to protect them from freezing in the water. But these factors are not an advantage on land in the tropical heat.

These tropical penguins have, therefore, developed ways to survive the oppressive heat. The simplest of these is accomplished with their layer of fat, which contains a network of blood vessels. In cooler temperatures, these vessels draw together, and the layer of fat becomes thicker. But in warmer weather, blood flows freely through the vessels, carrying excess body heat to the surface, where it is released. The undersides of the wings also contain many blood vessels. When Galápagos penguins feel the heat, they stand with their wings spread out. In this way, excess body heat can escape into the air. The penguins' feet also help regulate body temperature. Galápagos penguins always stand so their feet are in the shadows cast by their bodies. Therefore, the feet do not absorb heat from the Sun. The feet also release body heat into the air. The penguins lie down with their feet outstretched (exposing the bottom of the feet) to allow heat to dissipate. The penguins also have bare patches of skin on their faces that serve the same purpose.

Galápagos penguins shed all their feathers twice a year. The first molting period occurs just before the birds nest. This way, the adults' coats are sleek and fresh when it is time to feed the chicks.

Opposite: Iguanas and penguins live side by side on the Galápagos Islands.

Right: Penguins in tropical areas stand with their wings outspread to release heat. They also stand with their feet in the shadows of their bodies. This helps keep them cool.

The brooding period begins in May. Whenever possible, the birds seek out a shadowy area for their nests. These nests are not very substantial. The female lays two eggs, and these are tended by both parents.

Because of their difficult living situations, Galápagos penguins frequently abandon their

nests. If the weather during the incubation period is too hot, they will leave the eggs and flee to the cool waters of the sea. The eggs will be lost, but the penguins may soon lay more eggs. The warm El Niño ocean stream also affects the Galápagos Islands. When the food-filled Humboldt Current is displaced by El Niño, both the adult birds and their chicks are without food.

Rockhopper Penguins

Scientific name: Eudyptes chrysocome
Total length: 21.7 inches (55 cm)
Weight: 5.5 pounds (2.5 kg)

Rockhopper penguins are the smallest of the crested *Eudyptes* penguins that live on the various islands surrounding Antarctica. Although the *Eudyptes* penguins inhabit a wide territorial range, they are similar in their behavior and appearance. Only different head ornaments provide a sure way of identifying the species. The rockhopper has a brown headband that extends from behind the eyes into long, bannerlike gold-and-black feathers.

Rockhopper penguins inhabit steep slopes. They are able to climb high cliffs with their sharp claws. But they do not prefer steep areas. Whenever possible, they like to nest on level ground. But these areas are often already occupied by the two other, larger types of *Eudyptes* penguins — the Macaroni and erect-crested penguins. So the rockhoppers work their way through the tussock grass outside the occupied rookeries and establish nesting places on the slopes. Tussock grass can grow to a height of 6.5 feet (2 m). Rockhopper penguins form streetlike passageways through this forest of grass.

Well-fed male rockhoppers come from the sea onto land in mid-October. First, they reclaim their old nesting sites from the previous year. Battles often develop during this time. *Eudyptes* penguins, especially the males, are particularly aggressive. The tough little rockhopper penguins don't even shrink back from attacking humans to drive them away from the rookery area. They spring up in the air, peck at the intruder's arm, and don't stop until he or she has left.

When female rockhoppers return from the sea, they receive a warm welcome from their mates. Both partners perform elaborate greetings and mating rituals in order to get themselves in the proper mood for breeding. *Eudyptes* penguins are faithful to their partners and to their nesting sites. After spending the winter months separately in the sea, the pair will meet up again at their old nest. It is no small accomplishment for mates to be able to find each other amidst the noise and chaos of the busy rookery.

Both birds work together to build their nest. The female uses her breast to form a nesting cavity in the ground; the male looks for nesting material. The materials include tussock grass, leaves, sticks, bones, or pebbles. Two eggs, unequal in size, are laid in November. The female takes up the first round of nest duty. While the female incubates the eggs, the hungry male returns to the sea to eat his fill. But duty soon calls him back, for the chicks will hatch in December. Once hatched, the helpless chicks

Above, left: Rockhopper chicks live in groups but are fed only at their own nests.

Opposite: These rockhoppers show how they earned their name!

must be tended and kept warm for another month. During this time, the female looks for food while the male stays with the chicks.

Sometime in January, the chicks become more self-reliant. They leave the nest more frequently and gather together with other youngsters in crèches. At that time, the father birds can return to the sea to eat. The mothers will continue to feed the young birds until February. Then, finally, the molting season begins for the rockhoppers. When this time comes, they stay on land, standing around like half-plucked chickens while they wait for new feathers to grow in.

Fiordland Crested
Penguins

Scientific name: Eudyptes pachyrhynchus
Total length: 21.7-27.5 inches (55-70 cm)
Weight: 6.6 pounds (3 kg)

Fiordland crested penguins are the rarest of the *Eudyptes* penguins. Only between five thousand and ten thousand pairs breed on the southern and southwestern coasts of the South Island of New Zealand. These penguins cannot withstand high temperatures, so they nest in woods and hollows. Fiordland crested

penguins have a bright yellow band that extends from their beaks up over their eyes and faint white marks on their cheeks. The band forms a thick yellow burst of feathers above the eyes.

Unlike the other *Eudyptes* penguins, Fiordland crested penguins do not lay their eggs in the summer. They lay eggs in July, in the middle of the southern winter. The chicks are raised in the spring and have all their feathers by December. This is early summer in the Southern Hemisphere. The male and the female share the duties of tending the eggs and chicks. The male stays on land for forty days to mate and to take on the first round of nest duty. Then the female takes over, and the male returns to the sea to eat. But he must return to the nest for several weeks to guard the newly hatched chick. The Fiordland crested penguin lays two eggs, but only one chick is typically successfully reared.

Opposite: Fiordland crested penguins like to nest in natural hollows between tree roots. But these forested areas are increasingly rare.

Above: Male Fiordlands have thicker, larger beaks than the females.

Snares Island Penguins

Scientific name: Eudyptes robustus
Total length: 22 inches (56 cm)
Weight: 6.6 pounds (3 kg)

Snares Island penguins nest on Snares Island in southern New Zealand. A few birds can also be found on neighboring islands. The Snares Island penguin is slightly larger and has a thicker beak than the Fiordland crested penguin. The markings on the Snares Island penguin closely resemble those of the Fiordland, although the eye band is somewhat narrower, and the Snares Island penguin has a patch of bare pink skin at the base of its bill.

Astonishing as it may seem, there are three to six times more Snares Island penguins than Fiordlands. There are about 33,000 Snares Island nesting pairs, although their territorial range is not as great as that of the Fiordland crested penguins. However, Snares Island penguins are still rare in comparison to other *Eudyptes* penguins. All three of the *Eudyptes* penguins found in the New Zealand area — the Fiordland, Snares Island, and erect-crested penguins — amount to about 155,000 pairs. By contrast, there are millions of *Eudyptes* penguins on the islands in the Antarctic region, most of which are macaroni and rockhopper penguins.

After spending winter in the sea, the Snares Island penguins return to their rookeries. Nests are established under low bushes and in tussock grass. Many parent birds suffer from the heat during the nesting period, for there are only a few spots where nests can be protected from high temperatures. Often, the birds are forced to brood near colonies of New Zealand sea lions.

Females lay their two eggs in September. The total breeding and chick-raising period lasts until mid-January.

Macaroni Penguins

Scientific name: Eudyptes chrysolophus
Total length: 27.6 inches (70 cm)
Weight: 9.2 pounds (4.2 kg)

There are 11,500,000 nesting pairs of macaroni penguins. This species accounts for almost three quarters of the 16,000,000 total *Eudyptes* pairs. Macaroni penguins live on various islands off the coast of Antarctica. Their crest consists of long, yellow-orange feathers extending from a similarly colored spot on the forehead to the back of the head.

Macaroni penguins frequently live in rookeries together with other species of penguin, especially rockhoppers. But they also often share space with gentoos. As already mentioned, all *Eudyptes* penguins resemble each other in terms of behavior and appearance. But according to one of the laws of biology, it is not advisable for similar species to live in close proximity to each other. They would compete for food and space and be forced to aggressively fight each other for these essentials of life. So, biologists are interested in how the macaronis and rockhoppers manage to live together so peacefully. Researchers have discovered various tricks the birds use to keep out of each other's way. Macaroni penguins arrive at the rookery a month earlier than their smaller cousins and occupy all the flat brooding sites. When the rockhoppers arrive later, they take over the slopes. The month-long difference in brooding times has its advantages later as well. While rockhoppers are incubating their eggs, young macaronis are already being fed. And when hungry rockhopper chicks require the most food, macaronis are already fully grown.

There are also differences in sources of nourishment when the two species brood together. Both species eat mainly crustaceans — mostly krill. Krill makes up from 75 to 90 percent of their food. But when macaronis live together with rockhoppers, the macaronis also eat other foods. They eat twice as much fish and squid as the rockhoppers.

If they are in the process of gathering food, macaroni penguins remain at sea twenty-four hours a day. They look for schools of krill on the high seas and eat during the night. Gentoo penguins also frequently live with the macaronis. They seek their food far from the macaronis, mainly along the coastline.

The brooding habits of macaroni penguins correspond to other *Eudyptes* penguins. Males and females share the work of raising the young. Chicks are mature sometime in January, and, a month later, the molting period begins for adults. After this is finished, the macaronis will search for food again.

Above, left: *Macaroni penguins live on islands off of Antarctica.*

Opposite: *In the midst of chaos and noise, two penguins in the center raise their beaks and trumpet to announce they are mates.*

Royal Penguins

Scientific name: Eudyptes schlegeli
Total length: 24.5 inches (62 cm)
Weight: 8.8 pounds (4 kg)

like the macaronis. The royals brood in giant colonies on the Macquarie Islands. The female lays two eggs in a shallow nest made of small stones, clay, or bones. For five weeks, the parent birds take turns sitting on the eggs. After the eggs hatch, the chicks need to be protected for the first two or three months.

Royal penguins can be distinguished from their *Eudyptes* relatives by one obvious characteristic. All the others have heads that are mostly black, but royal penguins have white cheeks and a white throat.

Royal penguins raise their young much

As is the case for all *Eudyptes* penguins, the entire colony of penguins returns to the rookery each year. *Eudyptes* penguins are relatively late "bloomers," for they usually breed for the first time only when they are between seven and nine years old.

Erect-crested Penguins

Scientific name: Eudyptes sclateri
Total length: 26 inches (67 cm)
Weight: 8 pounds (3.6 kg)

Erect-crested penguins have a truly regal adornment on their heads. The bright yellow feathers extending outward above their eyes look like a crown. This species broods primarily on the Antipodes and Bounty islands in the Pacific Ocean.

When the erect-crested penguins return to land in September, the noise level in their rookeries is almost deafening. All *Eudyptes* penguins have rough, loud voices, but the erect-crested penguins are the loudest. *Eudyptes* penguins are more aggressive than most other penguins, and yet it is they that are most likely to live in overcrowded colonies. In addition, these are colonies in which several species of penguins sometimes live side by side. To keep misunderstandings to a minimum, these species developed a language of sounds and gestures. This language enables them to send signals to one another and to make their needs clearly known.

During the brooding period, erect-crested penguins must frequently cover a long distance on foot between the sea and their nesting sites. In so doing, they pass countless other nesting birds who greet passersby with only a threatening raised beak. Erect-crested penguins on their journey between the sea and their nest will hurry along through the rookery with their chests bent forward and their heads lowered. They will stop only briefly from time to time to look up and doublecheck to make certain they are headed in the right direction. With this style of travel, the penguins usually manage to make the trip unharmed. This behavior is also exhibited by the Adélie penguins, who live in huge colonies as well. Erect-crested penguins are

very vocal when they are at their nests. One first step toward the bonding of the pair is mutual grooming. This is followed by mutual bowing, looking up to the sky, and trumpeting. This behavior strengthens the pairs' sense of belonging to one another.

Above: Seals and penguins don't always get along. The New Zealand sea lion can be an enemy for erect-crested penguins.

Opposite: Many yellow-eyed penguins suffer from the heat because the forests that could provide them with shade are being cut down.

Yellow-eyed Penguins

Scientific name: Megadyptes antipodes
Total length: 26 inches (66 cm)
Weight: 11 pounds (5 kg)

Yellow-eyed penguins nest on the eastern coast of South Island of New Zealand as well as on the Auckland and Campbell islands. They live all year round in their rookeries, are fiercely independent, and live in widely scattered communities.

The winter season runs from April through August for the yellow-eyes. During winter, they spend each day in the sea, searching for food. They return to land to sleep only in the late afternoon. But this routine comes to an end in late August, when the nesting period begins. The pairs get together and choose a nesting site. Only about a third of them will use the same site as the year before. Yellow-eyed penguins are ground and burrow nesters. They build their nests between small, grass-covered spaces in the ground, under overhanging rocks, in flat hollows, or under roots. The female lays two eggs in October. Both birds take turns incubating the eggs until the eggs hatch after forty or fifty days. One parent bird then tends the chicks for another forty to fifty days, while the other goes out to hunt for fish or squid. After this time, the chicks still have to be fed, but they no longer need to be guarded. By March, they are self-sufficient.

Yellow-eyed penguins originally brooded in coastal forests of southern yew trees. There, they had protection from the heat. But yew forests have become rare in their brooding areas. Most of the forests have been cleared away for agriculture. Between 1948 and 1988, the numbers of yellow-eyed penguins decreased by up to 75 percent in some areas.

The yellow-eyed penguins have also suffered significant losses from predators brought to New Zealand by humans. During the penguins' nesting period, the chicks become a welcome treat for stoats, ferrets, dogs, and cats. In some areas, an entire rookery of chicks can be lost to these predators over the course of only a few weeks.

Little Blue Penguins

Scientific name: Eudyptula minor
Total length: 16 inches (40 cm)
Weight: 2.4 pounds (1.1 kg)

Little blue penguins have been appropriately named. They are almost three times smaller and thirty times lighter than the largest emperor penguins. In addition, their undersides are white, and their backs are bluish-gray.

There are four subspecies of blue penguin. The northern little blue penguins live on the southern and southwestern coasts of Australia as well as the coast of New Zealand. The southern little blue penguins live around the South Island of New Zealand and on several adjacent small islands. The Chatham little blue penguin is found on the Chatham Islands, and the white-flippered little blue penguin lives on the Banks Peninsula on the eastern coast of South Island in New Zealand.

The little blues are not travelers. They remain in their rookeries year round. Although they are coastal dwellers, their nesting sites are sometimes built up to .31 miles (.5 km) inland. During the day, they search for food in the sea. They return to their brooding hollows at night and travel again to the sea at sunrise. Their mating, nesting, and molting all take place in the privacy of their brood burrows. This is much to the regret of penguin researchers, who want to learn about the penguins' behavior.

Little blue penguins around New Zealand begin their mating season in April or May. Depending on the area, the penguin pair will live in a self-dug sand burrow or under thick plant growth. Sometimes they can also be found in groups in natural hollows in the cliffs. A single male attracts a female with an endearing mating call. These birds rarely fight with their neighbors. However, males living in a group perform a group mating call to attract the attention of single females. This behavior does sometimes lead to disagreements. Competition for a particular female can lead to aggression among the males. In addition, the lack of free space in these crowded dwellings can frequently lead

Above: This little blue penguin is surprised by a photographer as it makes its nighttime journey from the sea to its nest.

Opposite, left: A penguin feels at home only in the water.

Opposite, right: The nest of a little blue penguin.

to fights between families when the chicks are being raised.

The female little blue lays two eggs in September or October. One parent remains on land to incubate them. After about five weeks, two little blue-gray balls of fluff are hatched. These chicks immediately need to be kept warm. It will be two or three weeks before they are able to maintain their own body temperature. At this point, their parents will be able to leave them on their own for a day. While their parents are off fishing, the chicks huddle together to await the adults' return. The parents return after sunset and feed their offspring with small fish. The little blue chicks are mature fifty to fifty-five days after they hatch. No other penguin species raises its young so quickly.

The northern little blue penguins that live on the coast of Australia follow a somewhat different routine. Australian little blues live

farther north in a more temperate climate than their cousins in New Zealand. They have no set brooding season. Although most brooding takes place between August and January, researchers have found birds brooding all year round. Some pairs breed twice in one year, and a few even three times.

Many pairs succeed in raising all four chicks from two broods.

Little blue penguins can live to be quite old. Once a bird has survived the first five years, it can live to be as much as fifteen to twenty years old. But only about one-third of the birds survive their first year. Young,

inexperienced penguins on land risk being attacked by dogs, cats, weasels, and polecats. They can also be hit by trucks and automobiles, since many of the penguins must cross coastal roads on their way back from the sea to their nesting places. In the sea, they can fall victim to sea lions. But the penguins suffer most on account of humans. People clear away the bushes and trees in their breeding areas, making the area uninhabitable for the birds.

After the chicks are on their own, the adult birds spend six to eight weeks stuffing themselves with food in the sea. They eat so much that they sometimes increase their body weight by a third. This eating binge is followed by molting. The penguins molt between the end of January and early February. While they wait for new feathers, the penguins fast for two or three weeks. In the process, they may lose half of their total body weight.

Where Are the Penguins Headed?

Penguins are delightful. They have comic charm and rarely fail to bring a smile to our faces. We see penguin images everywhere — from stuffed animals to advertising to newspaper cartoons. They decorate umbrellas, calendars, and postcards. But we should not forget the real penguins in all of this. They are not having as much fun as their images suggest. One report from a journal for bird researchers reads as follows: "On the Falkland Islands, bored pilots have made a sport of flying low over penguin colonies to see how the thousands of penguins will all turn their heads either to the right or the left all at the same time. The game continues as the pilots fly lower and lower over the penguins' heads . . . the poor penguins . . . raise their heads higher and higher until they finally fall over on their backs."

As with every animal, penguins deserve our respect. We must do everything we can not to interfere in their struggle to survive. Humans must honor the rightful place of all Earth's creatures. It will benefit us all.

APPENDIX
TO
ANIMAL FAMILIES

PENGUINS

Distribution of Penguins

Emperor: Antarctica

*King: Staten, South Georgia, Falkland,
Marion, Crozet, Kerguelen, Heard,
and Macquarie islands*

*Adélie: The coast of Antarctica as well as
the islands of South Shetland, South
Orkney, South Sandwich, and Bouvet*

*Gentoo: Small islands near the coast of
Antarctica as well as the South
Shetland, South Orkney, South Georgia,
Falkland, Staten, Bouvet, Marion, Crozet,
Kerguelen, Heard, and Macquarie islands*

*Chinstrap: South Shetland, South Orkney,
South Sandwich, South Georgia, Bouvet,
and Heard islands*

*Magellanic: The southern coast of South
America and Tierra del Fuego as well as
Staten and Falkland islands*

*Peruvian: The southwestern coast of South
America*

Black-footed: The coast of southern Africa

Galápagos: Galápagos Islands

*Rockhopper: Tierra del Fuego as
well as the Falkland, Tristan da Cunha,
Gough, Prince Edward, Crozet, St. Paul,
Amsterdam, Kerguelen, Heard, Bounty,
Antipodes, Auckland, Campbell, Snares,
and Macquarie islands*

*Fiordland: New Zealand (the southern and
southwestern coast of South Island)*

Snares Island: Snares Islands

*Macaroni: South Shetland, South Orkney,
South Sandwich, South Georgia, Falkland,
Bouvet, Prince Edward, Kerguelen, and
Heard islands*

Royal: Macquarie Islands

*Erect-crested: Bounty, Antipodes, Campbell,
and Auckland islands*

*Yellow-eyed: New Zealand (the eastern
coast of South Island), the Steward,
Auckland, and Campbell islands*

*Little Blue: New Zealand (the South Island
and the Banks Peninsula), Tasmania,
the southern and southwestern coasts
of Australia*

Galápag

African penguin

rockhopper penguin

gentoo penguin

SOUTH AMERICA

Falkland

Staten

TIER

D

FUE

Peruvian penguin

Galápago

Magellanic penguin

king penguin

yellow-eyed peng

nguin

Tristan da Cunha

Gough

AFRICA

macaroni penguin

Prince Edward

Bouvet   **Marion**

Crozet

Adélie penguin

th Georgia

Kerguelen   **Amsterdam**

South Sandwich   **Heard**   **St. Paul**

outh Orkney

th Shetland

chinstrap penguin

ANTARCTICA

● **South Pole**

little blue penguin

Macquarie

Campbell   **Auckland**   **TASMANIA**

Antipodes   **Snares**

Bounty   **Stewart**

AUSTRALIA

NEW ZEALAND

erect-crested penguin

emperor penguin

royal penguin   *Fiordland crested penguin*   *Snares Island penguin*

ABOUT THESE BOOKS

Although this series is called "Animal Families," these books aren't just about fathers, mothers, and young. They also discuss the scientific definition of *family,* which is a division of biological classification and includes many animals.

Biological classification is a method that scientists use to identify and organize living things. Using this system, scientists place animals and plants into larger groups that share similar characteristics. Characteristics are physical features, natural habits, ancestral backgrounds, or any other qualities that make one organism either like or different from another.

The method used today for biological classification was introduced in 1753 by a Swedish botanist-naturalist named Carolus Linnaeus. Although many scientists tried to find ways to classify the world's plants and animals, Linnaeus's system seemed to be the only useful choice. Charles Darwin, a famous British naturalist, referred to Linnaeus's system in his theory of evolution, which was published in his book *On the Origin of Species* in 1859. Linnaeus's system of classification, shown below, includes seven major categories, or groups. These are: kingdom, phylum, class, order, family, genus, and species.

An easy way to remember the divisions and their order is to memorize this sentence: "Ken Put Cake On Frank's Good Shirt." The first letter of each word in this sentence gives you the first letter of a division. (The *K* in *Ken,* for example, stands for *kingdom.*) The order of the words in this sentence suggests the order of the divisions from largest to smallest. The kingdom is the largest of these divisions; the species is the smallest. The larger the division, the more types of animals or plants it contains. For example, the animal kingdom, called Animalia, contains everything from worms to whales. Smaller divisions, such as the family, have fewer members that share more characteristics. For example, members of the bear family, Ursidae, include the polar bear, the brown bear, and many others.

In the following chart, the lion species is followed through all seven categories. As the categories expand to include more and more members, remember that only a few examples are pictured here. Each division has many more members.

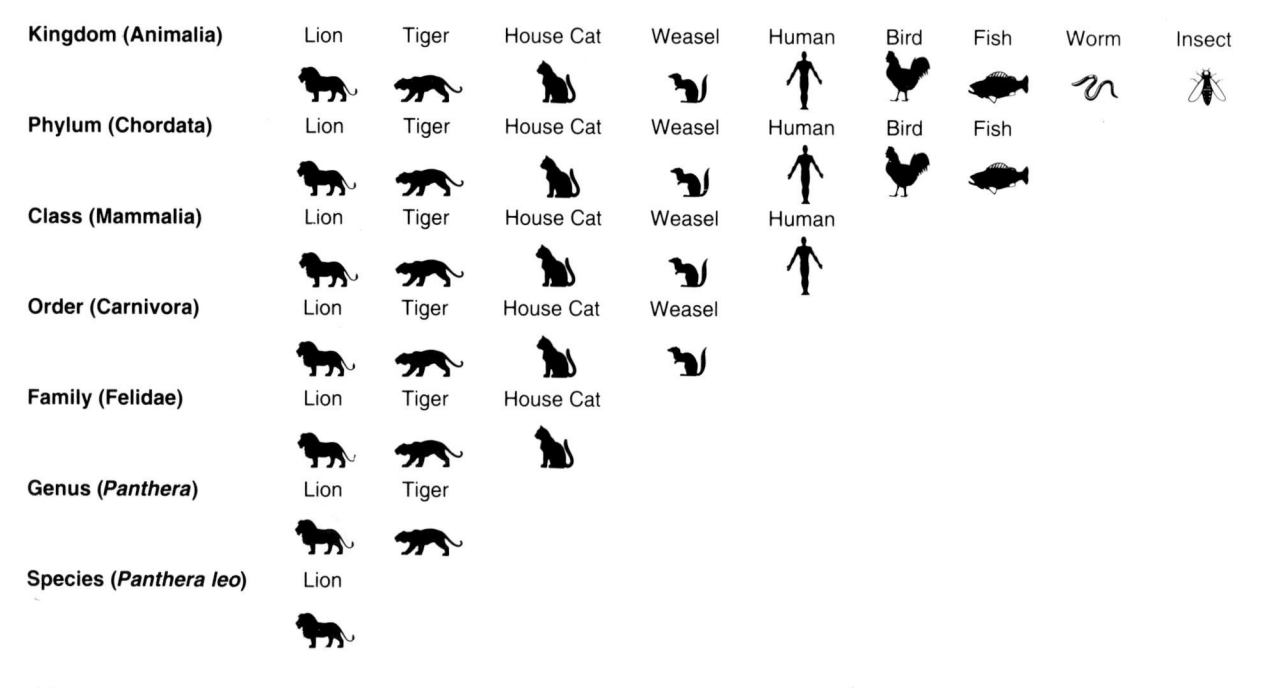

Kingdom (Animalia)	Lion	Tiger	House Cat	Weasel	Human	Bird	Fish	Worm	Insect
Phylum (Chordata)	Lion	Tiger	House Cat	Weasel	Human	Bird	Fish		
Class (Mammalia)	Lion	Tiger	House Cat	Weasel	Human				
Order (Carnivora)	Lion	Tiger	House Cat	Weasel					
Family (Felidae)	Lion	Tiger	House Cat						
Genus (*Panthera*)	Lion	Tiger							
Species (*Panthera leo*)	Lion								

SCIENTIFIC NAMES OF THE ANIMALS IN THIS BOOK

Animals have different names in every language. For this reason, researchers the world over use the same scientific names, which usually stem from ancient Greek or Latin. Most animals are classified by two names. One is the genus name; the other is the name of the species to which they belong. Additional names indicate further subgroupings. Here is a list of the animals included in *Penguins*.

Emperor penguin	*Aptenodytes forsteri*
King penguin	*Aptenodytes patagonica*
Adélie penguin	*Pygoscelis adeliae*
Gentoo penguin	*Pygoscelis papua*
Chinstrap penguin	*Pygoscelis antarctica*
Magellanic penguin	*Spheniscus magellanicus*
Peruvian penguin	*Spheniscus humboldti*
African penguin	*Spheniscus demersus*
Galápagos penguin	*Spheniscus mendiculus*
Rockhopper penguin	*Eudyptes chrysocome*
Fiordland crested penguin	*Eudyptes pachyrhynchus*
Snares Island penguin	*Eudyptes robustus*
Macaroni penguin	*Eudyptes chrysolophus*
Royal penguin	*Eudyptes schlegeli*
Erect-crested penguin	*Eudyptes sclateri*
Yellow-eyed penguin	*Megadyptes antipodes*
Little Blue penguin	*Eudyptula minor*

GLOSSARY

adaptation
The process of adjusting to a new use, condition, or life-style. Flippers and body shape show how penguins have adapted to living in an ocean environment. Over one million years ago, penguin ancestors had wings and could fly.

ancestors
People or animals from whom one is descended; a predecessor.

camouflage
The way an animal changes its appearance, hides, or disguises itself to look like its surroundings. Animals camouflage themselves both as a way of protecting themselves and as a way of sneaking up on their prey.

class
The third of seven divisions in the biological classification system proposed by Swedish botanist-naturalist Carolus Linnaeus. The class is the main subdivision of the phylum. Penguins belong to the class Aves. Animals in this class share certain features: they are warm-blooded, egg-laying, vertebrate animals covered with feathers.

clutch
The number of eggs produced or incubated at once.

colony
A group of the same kind of animals (such as penguins) living together.

El Niño
A warm, southward-flowing ocean current off the coast of Peru that causes damaging environmental and climatic disturbances every few years.

evolution
The gradual process of change that occurs in any organism and its descendants over time. Organisms evolve to survive the changes that can occur in climate, food supply, air quality, and other such factors.

family
The fifth of seven divisions in the biological classification system proposed by Swedish botanist-naturalist Carolus Linnaeus. A family is the main subdivision of the order and contains one or more genera. Penguins belong to the family Spheniscidae.

fledgling
A young bird that has grown its first feathers and has left the nest.

genus
The sixth division in the biological classification system

proposed by Swedish botanist-naturalist Carolus Linnaeus. A genus is the main subdivision of a family and includes one or more species.

habitat
The natural living area or environment in which an animal usually lives.

incubate
To warm eggs with bodily heat to promote the development and hatching of young. Penguin couples take turns incubating their eggs.

inhabit
To reside, dwell, or live in an area. The Magellanic penguin inhabits the southern tip of South America.

kingdom
The first of seven divisions in the biological classification system proposed by Swedish botanist-naturalist Carolus Linnaeus. Animals, including humans, belong to the kingdom Animalia. It is one of five kingdoms.

krill
Small, shrimplike creatures that live in the open sea.

mate (verb)
To join together (animals) to produce offspring.

migrate
To move from one region and settle in another periodically, often seasonally. Many penguins migrate from northern regions, where they spend the winter, back to the rookery farther south.

molt
To shed or change fur, skin, hair, feathers, or any outer layer from time to time. During the molting process, penguins shed their feathers one at a time.

nesting period
The time penguins and other animals spend sitting on the eggs of their young to hatch them.

nomadic
Wandering; moving from place to place. Some penguins have nomadic life-styles.

order
The fourth of seven divisions in the biological classification system proposed by the Swedish botanist-naturalist Carolus Linnaeus. The order is the main subdivision of the class and contains many different families. Penguins belong to the order Sphenisciformes.

phylum (plural: phyla)
The second of seven divisions in the biological classification system proposed by the Swedish botanist-naturalist Carolus Linnaeus. A phylum is one of the main divisions of a kingdom.

predator
An animal that lives by eating other animals. Young penguins are best protected from predators by staying together in groups.

prey (noun)
A creature hunted or caught for food. Some penguins spend the winter near their prey so food is easy to find.

primordial
Being or happening first in a sequence of time. Remains of primordial penguins that were more than 45 million years old have been found in the area around New Zealand.

rookery
A large breeding ground or colony. Some rookeries host up to a million birds in a crowded space.

species
The last of seven divisions in the biological classification system proposed by Swedish botanist-naturalist Carolus Linnaeus. The species is the main subdivision of the genus. It may include further subgroups of its own, called subspecies. At the level of species, members share many features and are capable of breeding with one another.

velocity
The speed at which something moves. Penguins can reach a velocity of several miles (kilometers) per hour.

MORE BOOKS ABOUT PENGUINS

The Adélie Penguin. Jennifer Dewey (Little, Brown)
The Arctic and Antarctica. Alice Gilbreath (Dillon Press)
Penguin. Caroline Arnold (Morrow Jr. Books)
Penguin. Lynn M. Stone (Macmillan)
The Penguin in the Snow. Doug Allan (Gareth Stevens)
A Penguin Year. Susan Bonners (Delacorte Press)
Penguins. Sandra Lee Crow (National Geographic Society)
The Whispering Land. William F. Russell, ed. (Crown)

PLACES TO WRITE

The following are some of the many organizations that exist to educate people about animals, promote the protection of animals, and encourage the conservation of their environments. Write to these organizations for more information about penguins, other animals, or animal concerns of interest to you. When you write, include your name, address, and age, and tell them clearly what you want to know. Don't forget to enclose a stamped, self-addressed envelope for a reply.

African Wildlife Foundation
1717 Massachusetts Avenue NW
Washington, D.C. 20036

Greenpeace
1436 U Street, NW
Washington, D.C. 20009

The Wilderness Society
900 17th Street NW
Washington, D.C. 20006-2596

Canadian Wildlife Federation
2740 Queensview Drive
Ottawa, Ontario K2B 1A2

The Nature Conservancy
1815 North Lynn Street
Arlington, VA 22209

THINGS TO DO

These projects are designed to help you have fun with what you've learned about penguins. You can do them alone, in small groups, or as a class project.

1. Make a penguin mobile. On a piece of poster paper, draw each kind of penguin in this book based on the descriptions of penguins provided. Cut them out and color them on both sides. Punch a tiny hole in the top of each penguin. Thread string through the hole and fasten with tape to a hanger. Hang the hanger from a lamp or other place where it will move freely.

2. Create a salt map of the Southern Hemisphere using 2 cups (.48 l) of salt, 1 cup (.24 l) of flour, and 1 cup (.24 l) of water. Poster paint or food coloring can be added to color the dough. When the map is dry, label the continents and countries. Indicate where each species of penguin belongs with small penguins you draw, label, and glue to toothpicks.

3. Visit the penguin exhibit at the zoo. Watch how they walk, swim, and groom their "tuxedos."

INDEX